IT'S OK TO WALK AWAY from…

From the Mistakes of Your Past,
Your Comfort Zone,
Your Lot and
Habits!
Your destiny may depend on it!

Dr. David Sola Oludoyi

Citation: **SHINING LIGHT GROUP 2005**, David Sola Oludoyi.
                   IT'S OK TO WALK AWAY ... From the Mistakes of Your
                   Past, Your Comfort Zone, Your Lot AND Habits. Your destiny
                   may depend on it! xiv + 81pp

ISBN: 1-59971-087-0

Published by: Shining Light Group
                   Copyright © 2005 Dr David Sola Oludoyi

Page Layout & Printing:
www.oriiz.com

FOREWORD

To walk means to move with your feet - putting one foot in front of the other and progressively moving in a certain direction. You can walk towards, walk into or walk away from something or someone.

As you open the pages of this book you are being invited to walk away from your mistakes, your comfort zones, your bad habits and your past.

You have an enemy called your past. Your past is an event or experience that has happened and cannot happen again.

Your past is an empty threat.

Your past is often the cause of regrets and setbacks.

Your past can kill your dreams, abort destiny and cripple progress.

Your past makes you think there is no tomorrow. However, you can have a future IF you're prepared to deal with your past.

Isaiah 43:18, 19 says: *"Remember ye not the former things, neither consider the things of old. Behold, I will do a new thing; now it shall spring forth".* Behold, look, see, I will do a new thing, not "I shall", or "I might", but I will (affirmative) do a new thing. To forget is a choice, a choice that releases you out of bondage and captivity and launches you into purpose and destiny.

"For I know the thoughts that I think towards you, saith the lord, thought of peace and not of evil to give you an expected end. God has good thoughts towards you, to give you a hope, a future, and an expected end." Jeremiah 29:11

Your present situation is not your final destination. The greatest enemy of your future is your past. The greatest enemy of your tomorrow is your yesterday. The greatest enemy of your destiny is your history, and the greatest enemy of your latter is your former.

In this book Pastor Sola endeavours skilfully, yet militantly to challenge and provoke you to come out of mediocrity, to refuse to settle for less and to walk into your destiny.

Destiny is of God, but the fulfilment of destiny is linked to another man. Every Joseph needs a Butler to lead them to their Pharaoh (prophetic destiny).

I believe that this book will serve as the spiritual catalyst to awaken those sleeping dreams, visions, gifts, innate potentials and aspirations that are deeply embedded in the innermost recesses of your spiritual wombs.

I celebrate you for choosing this book. Ingest it, digest it, assimilate it, summarize it, and then execute it!

Watch God turn your mess into a miracle and your mistakes into a ministry.

This is the place in God where your expectations become manifestations.
May your expectation never be cut off!

Fulfil your destiny!

Pastor Sarah Morgan
Vision International Ministries
Los Angeles, California USA

ACKNOWLEDGEMENTS

Whenever one stops learning, one stops growing. A person that never refers to another could never be a reference.

I am forever grateful to my numerous teachers and instructors whose dedication and passion keeps inspiring me.

Yvonne Raynor is a gifted, dedicated, and diligent editor who advised and worked with me to deliver this book: You are a blessing.

The relentless and hard working SLG team, despite all, you are still standing, I salute you.

My loudest cheering team: Sade, Enoch-David, and Mary-Grace - what a privilege to father you all.

My brilliant, organised and exceptionally intelligent wife, Grace-Sola, and therefore my most significant cheerleader: You taught me to walk away from the old to walk into the new.

To RCN Pastors thanks for being there.

DEDICATION

To all who are going through issues that appear un-resolvable: To those who are in the valley of decisions: To all those who have embarked on the journey of life and yet found your destinations seem so far away,

To the unsung "hero" who has dealt with challenges, is dealing with challenges and will yet deal with more challenges,

To the countless millions who need to leave something behind,

ARISE and SHINE!

Get ready to put on your shoes, and tighten your belts, because you will walk into a NEW beginning in Jesus' name.

CONTENTS

INTRODUCTION

It is spiritually and physically possible to walk away from all that you have ever known. The children of Israel had to leave Egypt before they could enter the Promised Land. They could not take the baggage of the past with them.

A delayed or aborted destiny often result when you don't walk away from individuals or the past. Environments or people can't stop you experiencing new beginnings but your mindset can. God is progressive; and is continuously doing new things; as he made you in his image, it's likely he wants you to follow suit.

If you refuse to cooperate, his plans and purposes will still be accomplished one way or another, but some of you may just end up old, and grey-haired and always complaining: you know I could have been this but... Or, I could have been that but...

You can still change your testimony. Don't let regret, remorse or reproach cheat you anymore. You may think God's promises have failed to manifest in your life but Psalm 93:5 tells us that his "testimonies are very sure..."

God's mercies are new every morning (Lamentations 3:21-23). Hebrews 6:9 says, *"But, beloved, we are persuaded better things of you, and things that accompany salvation, though we thus speak."*

God may not bless you where you are now because your destiny is tied to a designated location on this earth.

It's not too late to find that destiny.

This book is about new beginnings.

It was written to encourage you to have hope when all hope has gone.

"So don't lose your confidence. It will bring you a great reward."
Hebrews 10:35

Chapter 1

WHAT WILL YOU WALK AWAY FROM?

At some point in your lives, God will call you to walk away from something or someone before you can walk into his promises. The spiritual precedent was set when God told Abram to walk away from all that he had known.

Leave home? Leave all my relatives? And all that is familiar to me? No way, I must be hearing things…

Genesis 12:1-4 says, *"Now the Lord had said unto Abram, Get thee out of thy country, and from thy kindred, and from thy father's house, unto a land that I will show thee:*

And I will make of thee a great nation, and I will bless thee, and make thy name great; and thou shalt be a blessing:

And I will bless them that bless thee, and curse him that curseth thee: and in thee shall all families of the earth be blessed. So Abram departed, as the Lord had spoken unto him; and Lot

3

went with him: and Abram was seventy and five years old when he departed out of Haran."

It may sound foolish to you (and to others!). God's instruction may have sounded absurd to Abram, but most importantly, he obeyed. In fact, God's instructions always sound foolish. It was while trusting God for a new church building that, in the middle of a worship service, the Lord suddenly revealed he wanted certain people to donate £500. I hadn't planned to take up an offering, but blindly obeyed him and announced his words to the congregation.

As one or two people raised their hands, God immediately told me to tell them, he was only testing their obedience, and that they should keep their money. Later one of them came back to testify how after leaving the church, he'd been blessed with some money by someone who'd been unaware of his desperate need. God always delights in rewarding your instant obedience with double blessings!

So, if you're unwell and someone prays for you: believe you've been healed. Take a step of faith and do what you couldn't before. It might be painful at first but your body will gradually strengthen as you keep persevering. Don't wait for the symptoms to disappear before exercising faith. Don't wait around for the approval of others before acting on God's word, because a day will surely come when you let them down and they walk away.

You need to understand that you don't live to please others, and this includes the misguided Christian folk that believe unity only lasts as long as we all stay in church together, and who tolerate or greet you because you attend church.
It takes blind faith to set out on an unknown journey. Abram

didn't know where he was going. He'd never done anything like this on his own before.

Yet he obeyed without knowing the bigger picture.

He obeyed without knowing all the logistics.

He obeyed without asking what ifs.

He obeyed without doubting.

What is God telling you to walk away from?
Is it something you've struggled with all your life?

Is it a cross you've been bearing that God didn't give you?

Is it private demons like bad behaviour?

Self-control?

Self-reliance?

Is it unfaithfulness towards God?

Or, is it … (you can fill in the blanks)?

We like to be real with others, but some of us need to be real with ourselves, too.

Abram previously only left his birthplace with his family to resettle in Ur of Chaldees, but after his father's death, God told him to move on and leave all behind (Genesis 11:31, 32). There was no time to grieve. Jesus realised his mother and disciples would mourn his death, as he hung on the

Cross, yet he also understood that the entire human race would mourn if he disobeyed his Father's will. So, simply, he said, *"Not my will, but thy will be done"* (Matthew 26:39).

Can you echo his words?

During personal bereavement God will often talk to us about the future. *"And after the earthquake; a fire, but the Lord was not in the fire: and after the fire a still small voice"* (1 Kings 19:12). Amid the weeping and the condolences, listen out for his still, small voice.

There's an important message in Lazarus' experience (please read Luke 16:19-31). He was humble and impoverished and went to heaven, unlike the rich man who didn't have time for people like him and ended up in hell. As it was too late for his own salvation, he acknowledged that his living relatives still had a chance, and wanted Lazarus sent to his family to tell them to stop grieving over his death, to repent and sort out their lives so that they wouldn't join him in hell.

It's not too late for you to stop grieving and enter new beginnings.

Now let's break down God's instructions to Abram: "Get thee out of thy country..."

Country means territory. All Abram's interests were in Haran. He had grown used to a certain lifestyle only for God to reveal that although he'd done really well, Haran wasn't where he'd fulfil destiny. He had bigger plans for him.

God wants to move you out of a spiritual territory. Is it your workplace, household, or comfort zone? Perhaps God wants you to leave the cosy job for one that might stretch you. The Lord works in mysterious ways only to whom the gospel is hidden (2 Corinthians 4:3), as Ephesians 1:19 says, *"Having made known unto us the mystery of his will, according to his good pleasure which he hath purposed in himself."*

God will tell you to walk away from something for very good reasons. Jesus only fulfilled his destiny after moving away from his birthplace. Even when he went back he wasn't able to perform any miracles because familiarity can breed contempt. Some friends or family will never accept you've become a new person in Christ. Even when your inner transformation can be plainly seen, they'll still look at you, and say, so what? Didn't we know you before?

Stop fighting your battles (1 Samuel, 17:47). Stop trying to change their opinions, which they're entitled to anyway. 2 Corinthians 4:13 says, *"But if our gospel be hid, it is hid to them that are lost."* You can't make them understand your vision. Remember Joseph tried and look where it got him (read Genesis 37).

"And from thy kindred…"

The Oxford compact English dictionary describes kindred as:

1)   One's family and relations.
2)   Relationship by blood.

But God's not telling you to dump your family. Spiritual issues are being addressed when he tells you to let go of relationships with unbelievers or idolaters, that'll drag you down to their levels. I'm talking about those friends you knew before your conversion, who still haven't become enlightened. Two Corinthians 6:14-17 says, "Stop forming inappropriate relationships with unbelievers. Can right and wrong be partners? Can light have anything in common with darkness? Can Christ agree with the devil? Can a believer share life with an unbeliever?

The Lord says, 'Get away from unbelievers. Separate yourself from them. Have nothing to do with anything unclean. Then will I come unto
you' "

Some people are always scared of change, even when God has promised: *"Behold, the Lord thy God hath set the land before thee: go up and possess it, as the Lord God of thy fathers hath said unto thee; fear not, neither be discouraged"* (Deuteronomy 1:21). You must be prepared to leave fear behind you.

We'll look at Abram's relationship with his cousin Lot (whom he grievously took along with him) in more detail in chapter three but note what happened to Lot's wife after they followed Abram (Genesis 19). She looked back and instantly turned into a pillar of salt. Talk about spontaneous combustion. Always looking back destroys your life. You don't need to ask the next question. Lot survived to tell the tale, but had he looked back…

"Remember ye not the former things, neither consider the things of old." Isaiah 43:18

To remember is to bring something back to your memory, and relive or experience it again and again. If that's your problem, God is telling you to stop it, because a new beginning will never arise for you until you choose to stop rewinding the past.

Yesterday is past.

Today is a new day.

Often when we're in situations we don't understand our natural human tendency is to replay videos of the past but living in the past means that you can never enjoy what's going on now.

God is moving even now. Will you move with him? He goes on to say in verse19, *"Behold, I will do a new thing; now it shall spring forth; shall ye not know it? I will even make a way in the wilderness, and rivers in the desert."* You'll miss those new ways or quickly find yourself back where you came from if you don't let God change your mindset. May God help us in the name of Jesus.

"To everything there is a season, and a time for every purpose under the sun." Ecclesiastes 3:1

God wants to bless you, create a great nation out of you, and make your name great (Genesis 12:2). This is limitless and effortless blessing, with God's signature written all over it. You can't do it in your own strength. You need God's Holy Spirit inside you and empowering you (see John 14:26, 15:26, Romans 8:26, 27).

God wants to give you a new family, but he can't do that where you are. He will always do things differently to the way you would expect. Your cooperation is mandatory. Joseph had to move before he walked into destiny - and still it wasn't all plain sailing. A lot of the tough breaks included sibling abuse and wrongful imprisonment.

What hard knocks has life given you? Joseph didn't put up any struggle. He never defended himself, and went like a lamb to the slaughter. Ring any bells?

"He was oppressed, and he was afflicted, yet he opened not his mouth; he is brought as a lamb to the slaughter, and as a sheep before her shearers is dumb, so he openeth not his mouth." Isaiah 53:7

We must give Jesus back our lives because he laid his down for ours (Romans: 6:3). Philippians 3:10 says, *"That I may know him, and the power of his resurrection, and the fellowship of his sufferings, being made conformable unto his death."*

God knew what he created you to be. It is so much more than what you are now. Get to know him (Jeremiah 24:7), and intimately understand his ways. Moses achieved that, and look what God said about him in Deuteronomy 34:10, *"And there arose not a prophet since in Israel like unto Moses, whom the Lord knew face to face."* It is still possible, however to get up close and personal with him, if you're willing to seek him with all your heart and soul (Deuteronomy 4:29).

Once he has your trust, he'll take you to the next level. He'll make your name great. If evil was said about you in the past – from now on only good will be heard about you.
So what are people saying about you?

Your name is only great when your work outlives you. God is saying that he is going to do the improbable in your lives. Where men said no way—God is saying I WILL MAKE

A WAY (Isaiah 42:16). The Lord is saying you'll have children; I'll bless you and make you prosperous, progressive and happy.

Do you want your name to go down in history?

What God accomplishes in you will exceed generations. John 37:8 says, *"He that believeth on me, as the scripture hath said, out of his belly shall flow rivers of living water."* You're never really blessed until your life is a blessing to others meaning that the blessings God bestows upon your life must flow out to others. If people saw you as a problem, instead you'll become a blessing. Many die without leaving a mark because their lives weren't useful to others, but God is saying, what I'm going to do in your life will make your name go down in history.

God says vengeance is mine (Romans 12:9). Once you know how blessed you are in Christ, you won't fight people anymore, you'll bless them, (Matthew 5:44). The covenant of blessing (Genesis 17:2, 7) also provides spiritual protection (see Job 1:10, Psalm 91) over your life so you don't need to worry if anyone tries to put curses on you. Genesis 20 gives a good example of God fighting for his people when a king unwittingly attempts to take Abram's wife. Your enemy's evil schemes against you will snare them while you remain blessed (Psalm 54:4, 121:7).

Your name will be remembered for good. People praying for you will be blessed. Wherever your name is mentioned, God will show up for you in Jesus' name. Henceforth, anyone who blesses you will be blessed (Genesis 12:3). Potiphar showed unusual favour towards Joseph and God blessed him (Genesis 39). Anyone who favours you will provoke favour from God. That's why Luke 6:38 says, *"Give, and you will receive. A large quantity, pressed together, shaken down, and running over will be put into your pocket. The standards you use for others will be applied to you."*

Chapter 2

IT'S MAKE OR BREAK!

Does your life seem as if it couldn't get any better because of what you've already achieved? While in Haran, Abram thought the same, too. The fishermen Jesus called in Matthew 4:18 thought they were at the right place but what they had accomplished just turned out to be just training for their true vocations, as Jesus told them (verse 19), *"Follow me, and I will make you fishers of men."*

You'll walk in your true purpose when you're willing to follow Jesus all the way. Jesus said I am the way, the truth, and the light (John 14:6).

"Before I formed thee in the belly I knew thee; and before thou camest forth out of the womb I sanctified thee, and I ordained thee a prophet unto the nations." Jeremiah 1:5

Jesus is saying follow me and I'll make you. Often we try to do it ourselves but end up broken. Total surrender to God enables you to overcome anything, and be strong and qualified for mighty exploits (Daniel 11:32b).

It's make or break time.

You'll make it if you let God plant you where he wants, and be willing to follow his directions. Job 22:2 says, *"Acquaint now thyself with him, and be at peace: thereby good shall come unto thee."*

Give God your undivided attention, and you'll become what he made you to be. If you're not prepared to completely follow Jesus, he can't make you. He won't be able to fulfil his best for you.

Do you think it's too late to change? I've got good news for you. Even the people who may have looked at you and said, you can't make it, can't stop you if you listen to God. Acts 5:29 says we ought to obey God rather than men, but that will make you very unpopular.

They'll think you're crazy yet who'd have thought a day might dawn when preaching the gospel could result in 3000 conversions as it did for Peter? He only made it once he decided to forsake all and follow Jesus. Judas was one of the 12 disciples whose unwillingness to follow Jesus, cost him his life.

Your life will not be lost in Jesus' name.
Let your prayer be: I will follow Christ, and he will make me because when he makes me no one can break me. When he lifts me up, no one can put me down. When he blesses me, no one can stop it. I'll follow him faithfully and he will make me.

Amen.
Follow Jesus, and just like he told Abram, he'll make you a great nation. He'll make you fishers of men. Make means to

manufacture. He'll make something out of you.

It doesn't matter where your life is right now.

It doesn't matter what your circumstances say:

Or what people say,
What your examination results say,
What your past says,
What your age says,
Or what mistakes you've made.
If you're willing to walk away from failure, self-pity and complacency, God will assemble your life again.

"To appoint unto them that mourn in Zion, to give unto them beauty for ashes, the oil of joy for mourning, the garment of praise for the spirit of heaviness, that they might be called trees of righteousness, the planting of the Lord, that he might be glorified." Isaiah 61:1

Genesis 1:1 says that in the beginning God created the heaven and the earth. In verse 26, he says, *"Let us make man in our image, after our likeness."* Isaiah 64:8 tells us that we are the clay and God is the Potter.

"Arise, and go down to the Potter's house, and there I will cause thee to hear my words.

Then I went down to the Potter's house, and, behold, he wrought a work on the wheels.

And the vessel that he made of clay was marred in the hand of the Potter: so he made it again into another vessel, as seemed good to the Potter to make it.

17

O house of Israel, cannot I do with you as this potter? saith the Lord. Behold, as the clay is in the Potter's hand, so I do in my hand, O house of Israel." Jeremiah 18:2-6

Have bitterness, vengefulness, and idolatry, or carnality marred your life? If you're willing to seek God above all else, not only will you see new visions but you'll have new purpose too (Romans 8:28).

Don't view your age as a barrier. Your spiritual progress isn't determined by age but by how much your life is surrendered to God. Abram was 75 years old when he started a new life in Canaan. At 60, Benjamin Franklin was a newspaperman, and by 81 he was framing the US Constitution. Golda Meir was 71 when she became the Israeli Prime Minister. George Bernard Shaw was 95 years old when his first play was produced.

What counts is what you do, not when you do it.

So God can still achieve wonders through you, whether you're aged seven, seventeen or seventy. But it's true to say that God always looks to the future when he wants to start something new and tends to choose young blood. Abram was the youngest among his brethren (check the facts between Genesis 11:26, 28, 32; 12:4), other examples can be found in the Old Testament i.e. Isaac, Jacob, and Joseph.

Sheer determination and tenacity will get you the impossible. This country might be economically good for Y and yet the opposite for X. It's the resolution to succeed that's important more than any thing else. Only those who really want to go far will find the way to do it, whereas people who don't always find excuses.

Abram made up his mind to obey God. Philippians 4:13 says, *"I can do everything through Christ who strengthens me."* You will be empowered to carry out God's will. Matthew 11:12 says, *"And from the days of John the Baptist until now the Kingdom of Heaven suffereth violence, and the violent take it by force."* It's time to press forward, like a soldier of Christ. Psalm 81:10b says, *"Open thy mouth wide, and I will fill it... but my people would not hearken to my voice; Israel would have none of me.*

You must press. Send out as many CVs as possible if you're looking for a job. God's grace and unmerited favour will make a way for you.

God is sending out a clarion call today. Will you heed that call?

Will you let fear go and act in faith? Are you prepared to face the unknown—prepared to face rejection, and keep pressing even after you've sent out 50 CVs, and can't seem to get a job?

Don't be lazy or lily-livered. Don't spend all day in front of the TV set. Get off your butt; get off your bed and pray. Jesus told his hired workers: *"Occupy till I come"* (Luke 19:13).

In John 14:12, Jesus says we will do greater works than he did. Discover what greater works you've been called to do, and get on with it. It might be nonsense to you but this is the season of foolish instructions. Step out in faith and God will see you through.

In the Old Testament, many past champions pressed, so

how much more do you and I, even in this dispensation of grace? In the book of Esther, Queen Vashti occupied Esther's position. Vashti had to be displaced - that meant Esther had to be willing to lose her life and to spiritually take what the Lord had already given her. Haman, the chief minister to King Ahasuerus, was the giant blocking that transition, which would change many other destinies, too. *"For though we walk in the flesh, we do not war after the flesh. (For the weapons of our warfare are not carnal, but mighty through God to the pulling down of strongholds)."* 2 Corinthians 10:3, 4

The people occupying your place will never willingly surrender their positions; so expect a fight wherever God sends you. If Jesus had to fight to the death, you will too. The battle's half won anyway because just before his Crucifixion, Jesus declared triumphantly, *"It is finished"* (John 19:30). Haman eventually fell on his own sword. There are careers out there, which you need to put in the spiritual effort to take back. God's given us promises in his word but only faith can activate them.

Satan occupied this earth until Jesus took back the keys to heaven and hell from him (Revelations 1:18). Luke 12:2 says, *"Fear not, little flock; for it is your Father's good pleasure to give you the keys to the kingdom."* Isaiah 22:22 says of Jesus: *"...So he shall open, and none shall shut; and he shall shut, and none shall open it."*

Once God opens a way for you, nothing and no one can shut it except your pride, envy or unbelief. Press on, and see your lives change for the better.

The way you speak will change.

The clothes you wear will change.
Your relationships will change.
Your attitude will change.
The way you've always thought will also change.

Philippians 2:5-11 says, *"Let this mind be in you, which was also in Christ Jesus: Who, being in the form of God, thought it not robbery to be equal with God: But made himself of no reputation, and took upon him the form of a servant, and was made in the likeness of men:*

And being found in fashion as a man, he humbled himself, and became obedient unto death, even the death of the cross. Wherefore God also hath highly exalted him, and given him a name which is above every name: That at the name of Jesus every knee should bow, of things in heaven, and things on earth, and things under the earth; And that every tongue should confess that Jesus Christ is Lord, to the glory of God the Father."

Verses 13-16, assures us that God is at work in you now both to will and to do of his good pleasure. He wants you to obey everything he says, without grumbling or arguing, so that you may be blameless and harmless: the sons and daughters of God without rebuke. In the midst of a crooked and perverse nation among whom you shine as lights in the world. Holding forth the word of life, that you may rejoice in the day of Christ, that you have not run in vain, neither laboured in vain.

God's saying that humility comes before honour; so for you to get a testimony, you've got to expect to be tested first. Acts 5:41 says, *"And they departed from the presence of the council, rejoicing that they were counted worthy to suffer shame for his name."*

Will you be counted worthy to suffer shame for Christ's sake?

You were created for glory (Isaiah 43:7). You'll become a thing of beauty (Psalm 50:2) in Jesus' name.

Chapter 3

DON'T BE CONTENT
WITH YOUR LOT

"Now there is at Jerusalem by the sheep market a pool, which is called in the Hebrew tongue Bethesda, having five porches. In these lay a great multitude of impotent folk, of blind, halt, withered, waiting for the moving of the water. For an angel went down at a certain season into the pool and troubled the water; whosoever then first after the troubling of the water stepped in was made whole of whatsoever disease he had. And a certain man was there, which had an infirmity 30 and eight years. When Jesus saw him lie, and knew that he had been now a long time in that case, he saith unto him, Wilt thou be made whole?" John 5:2-6

Imagine going to your doctor seeking a cure to your physical symptoms, but after you've told him your problem, the last response you expect to get is: "Would you like to get well…?" Well, ye-es, otherwise I wouldn't be here, would I?

You may just be surprised to learn that some people don't want to get better even if they profess they do. They have learnt to live with their spiritual lot when actually God wants to remove LOT from their lives.

25

Have you been told that's your lot in life?

Does your circumstances tell you that's your lot in life?

Have you said that's my lot?

God is saying: LET GO OF LOT.

Your Lot can be human.

Departing from Haran, Abram unwisely took along his cousin Lot. But when God wants to do a new thing in your life, there must be no hangers on. Matthew 9:17 says, *"Nor do people pour new wine into old wineskins. If they do, the skins burst, the wine runs out, and the skins are ruined. Rather, people pour new wine into fresh skins, and both are saved."*

So Abram didn't quite leave his past behind. Ostensibly, he didn't do anything wrong, and was just looking out for a cousin who'd also lost his father. But Abram was asking for trouble because Lot brought a lot more baggage than he did. He brought avarice and discord.

Genesis 13:7a goes on to say, *"And there was a strife between the herdmen of Abram's cattle and the herdmen of Lot's cattle."* Abram was soon forced to choose between his future and the past. In verse 8, he invites Lot to walk away, and thankfully he does.
But if people don't like your decisions such splits don't always end so amicably. They may not want to talk to you ever again, but God's will is more important than their feelings. Christianity makes no allowances for sentimentality. It's all about obeying God, and following tough decisions through.

You must seriously pray before inviting strangers into your households. Some of you let them into your households, without knowing their backgrounds, only to find sudden tension in the atmosphere. Strangers can introduce calamity into your life—and suddenly nothing works anymore, leaving you wondering what's happening to my finances, my marriage? - The answer's simple, you brought Lot into your homes.

Your Lot may try to follow you into the new thing that God wants to do, but ask God to give you the grace to overcome the fear of letting people even if they were dependent on you, or vice versa, walk away.
You have to let Lot sort out his or her own life. That also means letting your spouses sort out his or her own life. When we stand before God's judgement throne, there'll be no more Mr and Mrs—you'll stand alone to answer for the decisions you made in your lives.

"Wherefore, my beloved, as ye have always obeyed, not as in my presence only, but now much more in my absence, work out your own salvation with fear and trembling." Philippians 2:5

Many of us try to resist completely obeying God's instructions, especially if it doesn't make sense. But even if today your life is like Abram's, God wants you to understand that he can make sense out of your nonsense in Jesus name.

Your Lot can be environmental.

Abram's father had relocated the family to an idolatrous country. But once Abram reached maturity, God told him I'm calling you to a place where you can serve me without evil or perverse influences around, where I'll plant new seed into your genes, so that an entirely new nation comes out of your loins.

Lot can be your mentality, or an attitude.

"If so be that ye have heard him, and been taught by him, as the truth is in Jesus, That ye put off the former conversation concerning the old man, which is corrupt according to the deceitful lusts; And be renewed in the spirit of your mind; And that ye put on the new man, which after God is created in righteousness, and true holiness." Ephesians 4:21-24

Get ready to let go of all those things that have stopped your testimony so far.

You can't be spiritually and physically healed unless you're willing to become like Christ.

"...The stone which the builders rejected, the same is become the head of the corner: this is the Lord's doing, and it is marvellous in our eyes." Matthew 21:42 (see also Psalm 118:22-24)

Men may have rejected you. God may seem have to rejected you (see Isaiah 49:14, 54:6, 7, 60: 15a) but Joel 2:25, 26 says, *"And I will restore unto you the years that the locust hath eaten, the cankerworm, and the caterpillar, and the palmerworm, my great army, which I sent among you. And you shall know that I am in the midst of Israel, and that I am the Lord your God, and none else: and my people shall never be ashamed."*

So will you be made whole?

Now?

God expects you to do his revealed will as soon as he calls you. The book of Jonah reveals the kind of horrors that can befall disobedient Christians. Abram obeyed the call of God instantly, but he'd have called a meeting to prepare his family first. The biggest problem in many homes tends not to be wives wanting to have their way but their husband's refusal to explain their visions properly.

"Can two walk together, except they be agreed?" Amos 3:3

Communication is crucial. It's impossible for your wife to accept your vision once you've made a decision. Everything the Lord tells you must be shared with her, otherwise if it turns out you don't share the same vision, you're just creating division.

"Therefore shall ye lay up these my words in your heart and in your soul, and bind them for a sign upon your hand, that they may be as frontlets between your eyes. And ye shall teach them your children, speaking of them when thou sittest in thine house, and when thou walkest by the way, when thou liest down, and when thou risest up." Deuteronomy 11:18, 19

This problem brought ramifications for mankind when Adam did one thing, and Eve, quite another. Had Adam communicated his vision adequately to his wife, she'd have rebuffed the devil when he questioned what God told her (see Genesis 2:15; 3:1-24)? Husbands: you should always attend church with your families and not leave them at home. Tell your children about God and include them in family prayers, or else you'll wonder why they become teenage tearaways.

Hebrews 11:8-10 says, *"By faith Abram, when he was called*

to go out into a place which he should after receive for an inheritance, obeyed; and he went out, not knowing whither he went. By faith he sojourned in the land of promise, as in a strange country, dwelling in tabernacles with Isaac and Jacob, the heirs with him of the same promise: For he looked for a city which hath foundations, whose builder and maker is God."

What are you looking for?

This is the best time to be alive in the history of the world as God promises that his people will arise a glorious church, but if you aren't seeking his kingdom (Matthew 6:33), you won't be able to overcome the calamities and great darkness that's coming.

Many Christians ignore God's call to move on, and stay too long in the wilderness, finding all sorts of excuses especially if life is easy for them. Paul, who previously persecuted Christians, says, *"But God, who appointed me before I was born and who called me by his kindness, was pleased to show me his Son. He did this so that I would tell people who are not Jewish that his Son is the Good News. When this happened, I didn't talk it over with any other person: I didn't even go to Jerusalem to see those who were apostles before I was. Instead, I went to Arabia, and then came back to Damascus"* (Galatians 1:15-17).

Paul wasn't a procrastinator. He didn't turn to fellow Christians or to other Ministers to interpret God's words. He didn't say to anybody: What should I do now? How do I know whether this is from God? If anybody told you to go and kill someone, that would definitely not be God speaking, but if the Lord tells you to go and witness in the street or to go and pray for someone you know, then you should obey that at once.

It's interesting that in most cases people will do their utmost to wriggle out of whatever God calls them to do, but when the devil calls them you can't get them off the podium!

Believe me, the devil won't tell you to pray and fast for your Pastor, so why do you want to go to someone else, saying, do you think God would actually tell me to do something like that? Your obedience equals unlimited blessings. You'll give rise to doubts if you start rationalising, and soon see your testimonies turn instead to sob stories.

If you've had enough of struggling or running away from his will, you can ask God's forgiveness right now, and pray for direction in Jesus' name. Ask the Holy Ghost to speak to your heart. Tell him to exchange your stony heart for a heart of flesh (see Ezekiel 36:26). Tell him you want to become receptive to his will.

Now thank him for answering you in Jesus' name.

Pray for every Lot that is associated with you to leave now in Jesus' name. Any Lot that is in your home, career, ministry must leave now in the name of Jesus.

Pray that the Lord would empower you if he has been calling you to move on. Ask for the strength and boldness to obey his instructions from now on. Renounce any entanglements in your life, every distraction.

Lay down your life as Jesus laid his life down for you. Tell him, yes Lord, wherever you lead I will follow. Ask for the grace to obey his foolish instructions in the name of Jesus.

Now worship him, and praise his holy name.

Rejoice. This is a new day for you.

Chapter 4

DON'T WANT TO BE VULNERABLE?
(Don't Read Any Further!)

"The thief cometh not, but for to steal, and to kill, and to destroy: I am come that they might have life, and that they might have it more abundantly." John 10:10

Self-preservation can be one of the biggest impediments to your destiny. A lot of you are trying to protect yourselves from being hurt because of disappointing past experiences. So you say to yourself, I will come to church, listen to the sermon, say my prayers and quietly slip out. But Christianity is not about being an exclusive island.

Your life is designed to be in relationship with others. When you're guarded, you lack joy. When you're joyless, you're miserable, so you can't attract others to Christ, which is your Christian commission. So what if someone messed with you? People messed Jesus up yet he kept going, and fulfilled destiny anyway. If you're going to achieve anything

35

in your lives, you must be prepared to let people mess you up and disappoint you. Just choose to get over it and move on.

God wants to put you in situations where you'll feel vulnerable, but difficulties arise when you don't crucify your flesh. Galatians 2:20 says, *"I am crucified with Christ: nevertheless I live; yet not I, but Christ liveth in me: and the life I now live in the flesh I live by the faith of the Son of God, who loved me, and gave his life for me."*

It is impossible to get on with everybody. Jeremiah 17:9 says, *"The heart is deceitful above all things, and desperately wicked: who can know it?"* As a pastor, I enter into relationships fully expecting people to potentially hurt me. And when they do—you know what? It doesn't cause me pain, because I just try to get on with my life. (John 2:25). Get scripture

Of course, I appreciate when people do me well, but if not, I know that as mere human beings, we all make mistakes from time to time. So I'll always choose to forget and move on. Whether I actually like you or your behaviour is immaterial. The point is that I choose to obey God's command to love unconditionally.

We can't overcome if we're still ruled by emotions. The complaining spirit that cries: so and so ignored me, so and so stepped on my toes, so I'm not coming to church again, so and so said they'd call me but they haven't so I won't trust anyone again, must die. Why don't you call them instead of whinging?

Some of you even grumble about your pastors, but do you greet him or her? Christianity's not about me: me: me. We all must die to something. A continuous harvest of souls has come from Jesus' death. John 12:23, 24 says, *"Jesus replied to them, 'The time has come for the Son of man to be glorified. I can guarantee this truth: A single grain of wheat doesn't produce anything unless it is planted in the ground and dies. If it dies, it will produce a lot of grain'."* To live abundantly and achieve success like Abram, you must let your feelings die, and let God's word produce spiritual life in you (see Galatians 5:22, Ephesians 5:9).

One Corinthians 2:9 says, *"But as it is written, Eyes hath not seen, nor ears heard, neither have entered into the heart of man, the things which God hath prepared for them that love him."* We wouldn't strive to hold onto things so much if we realised they couldn't compare to what God wants to replace them with.

God wants to substitute your fears and doubts with faith and courage (see 1 Corinthians 10:13). The devil doesn't want you to know these truths that would set you free, which is why he'll fight to keep you preoccupied with only those things your natural eyes see (read 2 Corinthians 4:18).

So, after you've completely surrendered your life to Christ, the devil will try to take it back but don't worry, Jesus has already prayed for you (see Luke 22:31, amplified version).

The Bible tells us of a perfect, God-fearing man who had it all but God still had more for him, after he suffered for a while (one Peter 5:10). Job was his name. We are told about his enormous wealth, and his large family, who he prayed for daily lest they had pride. Job 1:6-11 says, *"Now there was a day when the sons of God came to present themselves before the Lord, and Satan came also among them. And the Lord said unto Satan, Whence comest thou? Then Satan answered the*

Lord, and said, From going to and fro in the earth, and from walking up and down in it. And the Lord said unto Satan, Hast thou considered my servant Job, that there is none like him in the earth, a perfect and an upright man, one that feareth God, and escheweth evil? Then Job answered the Lord and said, Doth Job fear God for nought? Hast not thou made a hedge about him, and about his house, and about all that he hath on every side? thou hast blessed the work of his hands, and his substance is increased in the land. But put forth thine hand now, and touch all that he hath, and he will curse thee to thy face."

Satan wanted Job to lose everything he held dear and his salvation. His faithfulness and commitment were being questioned, so God had no choice but to test his true loyalties, although he knew Job wouldn't disappoint.

What are you holding onto that might cost your salvation? After the devil had finished with Job, he was left with nothing.

No family.
No business.
No home.
No health.
And: no respect.

All he could say was, *"Naked came I out of my mother's womb, and naked shall I return thither: the Lord gave, and the Lord hath taken away; blessed be the name of the Lord. In all this Job sinned not, nor charged God foolishly"* (Job 1:21, 22).

Unlike Job, are you blaming God for what you've lost?

Job's wife even urged him to renounce his integrity (Job

2:9), but he responded in verses 10-17: *"… What? Shall we receive good at the hand of God, and shall we not receive evil? In all this did not Job sin, with his lips."* As a result, the last chapter reveals that God restored Job twice over.

If the Lord is no respecter of persons (Acts 10:34), how much more is the devil? It doesn't matter who or what you are—you may say you've got nothing but if you're a born again, spirit-filled Christian, the devil's not only after your life but also your livelihood.

If the devil can rob you of your destiny, he has hit the jackpot. If you let God accomplish his plans and purposes in you, you'll become great, and fulfil what Adam and Eve failed to do when God blessed them, and said: "Be fruitful, and multiply, and replenish the earth, and subdue it: and have dominion over the fish of the sea, and over the fowl of the air, and over every living thing that moveth upon the earth" (Genesis 1:22).

Genesis 2:7 tells us that God breathed life into human beings, which is why you and I are alive. In fact, we were just dust. If the true source of life is living inside you, he'll give you life partners. Adam received a wife, after God gave him life.

Two Corinthians 2:11 warns us not to be ignorant of Satan's strategies. He wants to steal your focus from God so you miss his blessings. And we know the pain of what it's like to miss someone or something in our lives, when we are to blame; when we know God was about to move in our lives but then missed out because we focused on our circumstances, or what people said.

The first thing we tend to think about when God tells us to do something is 101 reasons why we can't do it. Nothing in life will ever be attempted if all possible objections are overcome. God requires total obedience.

Trust in God completely, and you'll find it easier to be obedient. Allow your will to be broken as a broken vessel is what he uses. In agriculture, corn and wheat have to be broken before they're planted into the soil to produce grain. God wants to break your stubbornness so that you're pliable, humble and obedient. You must be broken before he can use you effectively.

The Bible says that you're cursed if you trust in your flesh. *"Obedience is better than sacrifice,"* (says 1 Samuel 15:22). When you begin to obey God, you'll live purposefully. Once you understand that Jesus laid down his life so you could have a better one, you'll find purpose. John 10:10b says, "I am come that they might have life, and that they might have it more abundantly."

Chapter 5

NEW BEGINNINGS
(And Giants Too!)

God is a guide to those who obey him but many people don't step out by faith because they fear the worst. After Abram set out, he was not left to stumble about in the dark, God showed up on many occasions with words of encouragement.

Deuteronomy 17:6 says, *"Out of the mouths of two or three witnesses, shall he that is worthy of death be put to death; but at the mouth of one witness he shall not be put to death."* Matthew 18:16 says the same thing: *"Take with thee one or two more witnesses - that every word may be established".* If anyone offends you, try to talk to the individual as quickly as possible, but if that fails, look for two or three reliable witnesses to prove your case.

God affirmed his promise to Abram by saying, listen; I have

said it once, now I'm saying it again. In 2 Corinthians 13:1, Apostle Paul reminded the Corinthian church, it would be for a third time that he was coming to them with a word of warning.

As God showed up to increase and strengthen Abram's faith, he'll do the same for you in Jesus' name. Romans 10:17 tells us that faith comes by hearing, and hearing by the word of God. Not just by reading the bible alone but hearing the word of God in a Holy Spirit-filled church. Churches are very interesting these days, with all manner of attendees. Some come for social reasons, but God is only interested in progressive Christians.

Faith doesn't come by gossiping or by playing gospel music, but grows through listening to the preached word. Read the Scriptures aloud to yourself and your faith will grow as you hear yourself speaking. Listening to the bible on tapes or recorded sermons will also be of huge benefit.

"For therein is the righteousness of God revealed from faith to faith: as it is written, The just shall live by faith." Romans 1:17

In Genesis 12:7, God promises multiple blessings to Abram. Remember in verse one, he is told—go to a land I will show you, now, in verse seven, he's told not only will I give you this land but your children will inherit it too. Generations have lost countless blessings because their parents disobeyed God's will. What if Abram had refused to obey God?

Unless you give to God what belongs to him (your life), you can't receive from him what belongs to you. That's why God will move from showing to giving, in Jesus' name. Looking

44

at and tasting food are two different things. Likewise, window-shopping isn't as actually gratifying as making the purchase.

Hebrews 11:6 says, *"But without faith it is impossible to please him: for he that cometh to God must believe that he is, and that he is a rewarder of them that diligently seek him."* But you will not be rewarded until you exercise faith. May the Lord help us in Jesus' name. Matthew 19:29, 30, says, *"And everyone that hath forsaken houses, or brethren, or sisters, or father, or mother, or wife, or children, or land, for my name's sake, shall receive an hundredfold, and shall inherit everlasting life. But many that are first shall be last; and the last shall be first."* For all you're willing to forsake for God's kingdom, you'll receive a hundredfold back in this world.

Stop holding onto the things that you know the Lord wants you to leave behind and you'll receive a hundredfold in Jesus name. For example, the Lord may be ministering to you to give him your property, e.g. home or car etc, but are you presently resisting his will? Please understand that you'll only ever experience a hundredfold return when you're fully prepared to cooperate with him.

Don't become a Christian backbencher. Some Christians start well but end up falling behind carried away by the cares of this world. It almost happened to me. It wasn't easy for me to leave my profession to become a full-time minister of God. But I know I'll receive a hundredfold in this world, plus everlasting life in the world to come. *"Get wisdom, get understanding: forget it not..."* Proverbs 4:5

So what do you want to possess? Property? Land? Job? Do you want a new challenge in life, or to improve your marriage? You must understand what God has already given to you. In Joshua 6:2, God told Joshua: *"See, I have given into thine hand Jericho...."*

You must be able to see yourself with it before you handle it. You cannot understand what is to be liberated until you see yourself that way. You cannot understand what is to be blessed until you see yourself that way. Until you see yourself in your new profession, you cannot move from your old one.

So what can you see?

Years ago, sitting at the back of the church, I saw myself preaching on a pulpit. What you can't imagine won't manifest in your lives. 2 Corinthians 4:18 says, *"While we look not at the things which are seen, but at the things which are not seen: for the things which are seen are temporal; but the things which are not seen are eternal."*

So if you marry someone because of his or her physical look, don't expect that relationship to last unless you're prepared to find out what the inner person's like. You might marry a man because of his muscles but what will you do when they turn to fat?

The things we see are only temporary as things quickly change, and people change. You should ask yourself what's behind those glossy lips or bulging biceps? Sooner or later people's true characters manifest, and then you'll realise you've married a monster instead of a man, a 'harpy' instead of honey.

Lamentations 3:51 says, *"Mine eye affecteth mine heart..."*

What you see affects your heart, and what you incubate in your heart, determines what you produce. When you keep seeing failure or hopelessness, that's all you'll experience.

Be wary of the kinds of TV programmes and films you watch, instead, you should "focus on Jesus, the source and goal of our faith. He saw the joy ahead of him, so he endured death on the cross and ignored the disgrace it brought him" (Hebrews 12:2).

"And Abram took Sarai his wife, and Lot his brother's son, and all their substance that they had gathered, and the souls that they had gotten in Haran; and they went forth to go into the land of Canaan; and into the land of Canaan, they came. And Abram passed through the land unto the place of Sichem, unto the plain of Moreh. And the Canaanite was then in the land." Genesis 12:5, 6

Although their journey wasn't easy, they kept going anyway until they reached Canaan, where they met the Canaanites. Biblically, Canaanite signifies giant.

Would God really send me to a place inhabited by giants?

If it took only a boy to handle Goliath —and you don't get much bigger than that, you and I have nothing to fear. Some of you obeyed God and left home and country only to be confronted with giants. God wants you to see them as stepping-stones towards promotions.

God will allow several giants in your lives until you've developed spiritual muscles. People who exercise can't really flex their muscles until they go to the gym. So giants are an unavoidable part of the process of making you. God has not abandoned you; he just wants you to mature, spiritually.

Some of you might've expected marriage to solve all your problems, and instead you found giants. You may think you need someone else to complete you, but God alone does that. Singles who are yet to marry, take note: only God can make you a complete person. Adam was whole before God brought Eve into his life.

Sadly, some women don't have a life of their own without their husbands. But Christian women, your lives are now established in Christ. You are empowered to be fruitful helpmates to your husbands, not burdens.

Men, too, must have some source of livelihood to be considered marriage material; women therefore should always find out if the men they want to marry are spiritually employed. If the answer's no, then these men will be nothing more than spiritually bankrupt. God will only introduce a wife to Help fulfil your God-given goals. You need to know where you're going.

Zechariah 4:6 says, *"Not by might, nor by power, but by my spirit, saith the Lord of hosts."* The battle to get to your destiny has many giants along the way, but as the battle belongs to God (one Samuel 17:47), you have nothing to fear. Giants aren't designed to pursue you but are to toughen up your character.

One Peter 5:8 says, *"Be sober, be vigilant, because your adversary the devil, as a roaring lion, walketh about, seeking whom he may devour"*. Who ever told you that your Christian journey was going to be a bed of roses, lied, because on the road to success, there'll be obstacles. What ever the devil tries, through circumstances or others, you must decide that it's not going to affect you.

Overcoming Goliath made David. Resisting Potiphar's wife made Joseph.

Your future was made because Jesus resisted the devil's temptation in the wilderness.

Challenges will come your way, but they're just for a season. 2 Peter 3:8 says, "But, beloved, be not ignorant of this one thing, that one day is with the Lord as a thousand years, and a thousand years is one day.

The Lord is not slack, concerning his promise, as some men count slackness…"

Learn to appreciate the law of progressive advancement. You don't join a company today and become its managing director tomorrow. You don't graduate from school and on the same day buy a mansion. 2 Corinthians 3:18 says, *"But we all, with open face beholding as in a glass the glory of the Lord, are changed into the same image from glory to glory, even as by the Spirit of the Lord."* And Proverbs 4:8 says, *"But the path of the just is as the shining light, that shineth more and more unto the perfect day."*

Deuteronomy 7:21 says, *"Thou shalt not be affrighted at them: for the Lord thy God is among you, a mighty God and terrible."* God promises to gradually remove those giants occupying your life.

Don't tempt fate. What comes out of your mouth is either a curse or a blessing, therefore the importance of meditation can't be overem phasised. Habitually meditate on the bible, pray unceasingly (1 Thessalonians 5:17) and constantly appreciate God in your heart.

Outwardly speak God's words, and watch good results come.

I knew a sick person who was given some Scriptures to meditate on and continuously pray over, nine days later his life changed. Psalm 107:2 says, *"Let the redeemed of the Lord says so, whom he hath redeemed from the hand of the enemy."*

Even if you don't feel like it, constantly confess scriptures like, I am blessed, and, it is well with my soul (Genesis 12:13). It is well with all that pertains to me (2 Peter 1:3). I can never fail; Jesus is on my side, fighting my battle for me. Favour is on me. People are coming from all over the world looking for me, to be a blessing in the name of Jesus. The wealth of the wicked is being transferred to my pocket in Jesus' name. It is a new day for me. I am highly anointed.

I declare that my spouse is fruitful, in Jesus' name. I declare no more miscarriages, or barrenness in the name of Jesus. I am not discouraged but confident in the Lord that he's taking me somewhere and giving me land little by little. The joy of the Lord is my strength (Nehemiah 8:10). I am complete. I am made whole in the name of Jesus. I choose to believe what your word says about me, Lord and not what the devil says.

Thank you Father in Jesus name. Amen.

Chapter 6

STAND AND GOD WILL DELIVER

So what do you put confidence in? Philippians 3:3, 4 says, *"We are the (true) circumcised people (of God), because we serve God's Spirit and take pride in Jesus Christ. We don't place any confidence in physical things, although I could have confidence in my physical qualifications..."* Do you have confidence in God or your secular qualifications? If you're depending on the latter to get you to your ultimate destination in life, that is, heaven, then think again.

Your spiritual covenant with God is your qualification. The title deeds are your passport to Paradise not letters by your name, or the connections you have to influential people. These connections will eventually fail, whereas Ezekiel 37:26 says, *"Moreover, I will make a covenant of peace with them; it shall be an EVERLASTING covenant with them: and I will place them, and multiply them, and will set my sanctuary in the midst of them for EVERMORE"* (caps mine).

If you experience failure despite your spiritual warfare, it could be due to a lack of confidence in the Almighty. You may say, Pastor, I won't get the job because I don't have the qualifications but I say that confidence is the feeling you have without fully understanding how God will do it. You just know somehow that everything's going to work in your favour. The foundations for confidence are strength of character, hopefulness and peace, regardless of circumstances.

But what happens when you have done all to stand (Exodus 13:14a, Ephesians 6:13-18) with no apparent result? Will you throw away your confidence or still believe God? Hebrews 3:6 says, *"But Christ as a son over his own house; whose house are we, if we hold fast the confidence and the rejoicing of the hope firm unto the end."*

Surely no one's faith was tested more than Shadrach, Meshach, and Abednego? They carried their confidence into the fiery furnace and were unharmed by the fire (see Daniel 3:1-28). Abram is another example; he became a humble tenant in his new life despite having been a landlord in the old. Are you presently trusting God for accommodation? In Isaiah 65:22, God promises us that we will build and inhabit houses.

Daniel 11:32 says, those who know their God shall be strong and do exploits. Your day has come in Jesus' name. But the devil will mess with your hope, if you don't know God properly. You will not be tossed to and fro anymore in the name of Jesus.

If you truly know the God you serve, then you'll step out in faith, and see God work wonders for you. Please don't say you can't get a good job because you don't have the necessary documents. You just lack knowledge of how to go about achieving the impossible.

Don't cheat the system. You don't need to lie if you know God. Proverbs 23:7 says, *"For as a man thinketh in his heart, so is he...."* Sometimes it might seem as though your faith is being tested to its limits but you'll overcome in Jesus' name.

Does your story echo David's cries in Psalm 55:1-5? *"Give ear to my prayer, O God; and hide not thyself from my supplication. Attend unto me, and hear me: I mourn in my complaint, and make a noise; Because of the voice of my enemy, because of the oppression of the wicked: for they cast iniquity upon me, and in wrath they hate me. My heart is sore pained within me: and the terrors of death are fallen upon me. Fearfulness and trembling are come upon me, and horror hath overwhelmed me."*

David was just a happy sheep tender when he got the royal call from God that would transform his life. But from that moment all hell seemed to break loose, which must have shaken his nerves somewhat.

Have you been questioning what's been happening to you since God called you? King Saul, who David replaced, began pursuing him as an enemy. You need to know that if you're going to walk into new beginnings with God, you'll face the kind of scary situations that'll require even scarier confidence in God.

Maybe you're thinking things might be easier if you went to another town or country, but David's contemplation in the following verse should make you think again. "Lo, then would I wander far off, and remain in the wilderness. Selah. I would hasten my escape from the windy storm and tempest."

Once he entered Moreh (Genesis 12:6) Abram, on the other hand, might have said, Lord, perhaps you should have sent me to the neighbouring city. The people look a lot friendlier. For all his faith he may have been about to give up when he saw that his God-given dream looked very different in reality.

Have you ever encountered the dark night of the soul where all you hear is I must have heard wrong, or that you never heard from God at all?

What are the voices of doubt telling you: that you'll never get married? Never get pregnant? It's time to answer them back. At the time you're thinking of giving up God could speak to you again, like he did with Abram. Genesis 12: 7 says, *"And the Lord appeared unto Abram..."* When it seems as though you're down to nothing, God's always up to something.

When God appeared and gave you a vision that was only meant for your eyes and ears only (in other words, it was classified information), did you, like Joseph, blab to the whole world? (read Genesis 37)

Have you been waiting, and waiting and you feel like you're going backwards instead of forward, so much so that you've stopped believing the vision is possible now? Habakkuk 2:3 has a word for you: *"For the vision is yet for an appointed time, but at the end it shall speak, and not lie: though it tarry, wait for it, because it will surely come, it will not tarry."*

God is saying that vision will definitely manifest.

WAIT for it.
Expect it.
Anticipate it.

Regardless of what is going on around you, the devil can't stop it in the name of Jesus. But impatience and frustration can stop it if you let them get the better of you. I believe, God is speaking to someone right now, and saying: don't give up on that dream or that desire I gave you. I will bring it to pass.

Your level of obedience will determine when God next speaks to you. But did you obey him in the past? No? Don't worry, once you've repented and asked his forgiveness, God says, I will do a new thing.

"For the gifts and calling of God are without repentance."
Romans 11:29

From the moment you choose to obey, he'll speak to you and give you further instructions. Remember, God appeared again only after Abram obeyed. May God grant you the grace to obey him in Jesus' name.

Grace enables you to endure under pressure, and push on in the face of fear. Somebody once said, "Success is never final and failure is never fatal, it is courage that counts". In other words, if you fail today it doesn't matter - you'll stand up and be counted again tomorrow. It takes some courage to stand up again. And it takes even more courage to keep standing after being counted.
God will encourage you for the next stage of your journey.

Joshua 1:7 says, *"Only be thou strong and very courageous, that thou mayest observe to do according to all the law, which Moses my servant commanded thee: turn not from it to the right hand or to the left, that thou mayest prosper whithersoever thou goest"*

But how do you keep your vision alive? Just like babies are incubated in the womb for nine months, so your faith must nourish your vision. Habakkuk 2:2 says: *"And the Lord answered me, and said, Write the vision, and make it plain upon tables, that he may run that readeth it."*
Write your vision down and document your progress in a journal or diary. Note down every word you receive from a man or woman of God that speaks to your vision. As you walk with God, he'll reveal more as he did to others that went before you. But you've got to keep the faith no matter what.

Ephesians 6:13 exhorts, *"... and having done all, to stand"*. It's after your faith has withstood the test of time that you'll receive the blessing contained in the promise (Hebrews 10:36), and which Isaiah 60:1, 10-17 wonderfully encapsulates:

"Arise, shine; for thy light is come, and the glory of the Lord is risen upon thee... And the sons of strangers shall build up thy walls, and their kings shall minister unto thee: for in my wrath I smote thee, but in my favour have I had mercy on thee.

Therefore thy gates shall be opened continually; they shall not be shut day nor night; that men may bring unto thee the forces of the Gentiles, and that their kings may be brought.
For the nation and kingdom that will not serve thee shall perish; yea, those nation's shall be utterly wasted.

The glory of Lebanon shall come unto thee, the fir tree, the pine tree, and the box together, to beautify the place of my sanctuary; and I will make the place of my feet glorious.

The sons also of them that afflicted thee shall come bending unto thee; and all they that despise thee shall bow themselves down at the soles of thy feet; and they shall call thee, The city of the Lord, the Zion of the Holy One of Israel.

Whereas thou hast been forsaken and hated, so that no man went through thee, I will make thee an eternal excellency, a joy of many generations.

Thou shalt also suck the milk of the Gentiles, and shalt suck the breast of kings: and thou shalt know that I the Lord am thy Saviour, and thy Redeemer, the mighty One of Jacob.

For brass I will bring gold, and for iron I will bring silver, and for wood brass, and for stones iron. I will also make thy officers peace, and thine exactors righteousness.
Violence shall no more be heard in thy land, wasting nor destruction within thy borders; but thou shalt call thy walls Salvation, and thy gates Praise."

These words shall be your testimony in Jesus' name.

Chapter 7

STARVATION! NAKEDNESS! COMPROMISE!
(This Is What You're Signing Up For)

Many things could have tempted Abram to go back to what he'd left behind.

Comfort.
Security.
Family.
Food.
Businesses.

But not even the sight of the Canaanites could tempt him into turning back. Genesis 12:9, 10 says, *"And Abram journeyed, going on still toward the south. And there was a famine in the land: and Abram went down into Egypt to sojourn there; for the famine was grievous in the land." After God's reassuring words, Abram took time out to praise and worship (verse seven) before moving on towards the vision, perhaps expecting things to be easier now.*

In Haran, he ate as much as he wanted to and still had enough left over for tomorrow. Now, in the south, he couldn't find as much as a crumb on the ground. FAMINE? Perhaps the giants weren't so bad after all. It wasn't as though he just had himself to think about, but also "Sarai his wife, and Lot his brother's son, and the souls that they had gotten in Haran".

You need to know that when you're about to meet destiny, opposition will intensify. It is at the point of victory that you tend to be at your most vulnerable, but don't lose heart; this is when you should expect God to do the unexpected.

Did God direct you to take a particular job only for you to find yourself in trouble there? Or did he speak to you about a life partner, but since you put on the wedding ring, you're now longing to be single again?

But how could it happen?

Could God possibly have made a mistake?

Could you be feeling what Abram might have felt: But Lord, HELLO? Am I not serving you with my heart and soul, and forsaken all for you? Did you
really bring us here to starve to death? Don't I pay my tithes, Lord? Don't I give offerings, besides?

So what do you do when the adverse happens? When you've prayed, praised, and laboured?

How do you cope if you've studied hard for exams and, after

God told you were going to pass, failed dismally? Does it mean God is a liar? Does it mean that there's no God?

Believe it or not, he understands what you're passing through. By virtue of his covenant relationship with God, Abram still had to pass through (Genesis 12:6). Isaiah 43:2 says, *"When thou passest through the waters, I will be with thee; and through the rivers, they shall not overflow thee: when thou walkest through the fire, thou shalt not be burnt; neither shall the flame kindle upon thee."*

Alpha and Omega has no beginning or ending, and knows everything about anyone in the whole wide world. As the song goes: ***He's got the whole wide world in his hands..."*** God is omniscient, omnipresent and omnipotent. Nothing that's going on globally or domestically ever gets past his eyes (see 2 Chronicles 16:9, Zechariah 4:10). Daniel 4:25 tells us *"That the most High ruleth in the kingdom of men, and giveth it to whomsoever he will."*

God knows exactly where you are on planet Earth and has provided a way of escape for you, against all the odds. So this isn't the time to look back with a view to returning to your old address. It's a time to reorganise, instead.

Psalm 33:18, 19 says, *"Behold the eye of the Lord is upon them that fear him, upon them that hope in his mercy; To deliver their soul from death, and to keep them alive in famine".* God foreknew the southern region would become famine-stricken, and already put alternative measures in place for Abram as we'll later see. He knows that your famine is not unto death (John 11:4).

Even if people start talking about your downfall, you should

65

say like Job, God will lift me up (Job 22:1). Psalm 37:19 says, *"They shall not be ashamed in the evil time: and in the days of famine they shall be satisfied"*. May that be your testimony in Jesus' name. Be reassured that when the unexpected happens, God's on your side. He has your interest at heart.

But I don't have any clothes to wear - shall that separate you from God's love? My family's in distress - shall that separate you from God's love? Romans 8:35 says, *"Who shall separate us from the love Christ? Shall tribulation, or distress, or persecution, or famine, or nakedness, or peril, or sword?"* The word 'who' refers to a personality, so your famine can also be a human being or a spirit.

Abram was an obedient, faithful prophet serving God with his whole heart. He taught his household to serve God, prayerfully, also building an altar at which they would all worship. But for all that the adverse still happened. Bad things happen to good people, as we know.

At various times you may feel forsaken by God but the bible says differently (see Psalm 9:10), so be careful what you say. The children of Israel's discomforts caused them to curse God, and die. Exodus 16:2,3 says, *"And the children of Israel, said unto them, Would to God we had died by the hand of the Lord in the land of Egypt, when we sat by the fleshpots, when we did eat bread to the full; Ye have brought us forth into this wilderness, to kill this whole assembly with hunger"* (read also Numbers 26-35). Thank God for his mercies.

There are times when I wonder, Lord, can I continue? Do I have the energy or strength? Can I go on anymore when people just don't seem to appreciate my efforts? I just want to pack it all in. Lord, I have prayed for people and seen wonderful results but where is my testimony? How long am I going to have to wait in the queue? How long, Lord? I have prayed, and fasted for others, and I know everything's well with them. But I'm not superhuman; I have my own challenges too.

Abram might've said, Lord, I believe, but right now in the land of promise, just when everything seemed to be going well, all I can see is famine. Habakkuk 3:17 says, *"Although the fig tree shall not blossom, neither shall fruit be in the vines; the labour of the olive shall fail, and the fields shall yield no meat; the flock shall be cut off from the fold, and there shall be no herd in the stalls: Yet, I will rejoice in the Lord, I will joy in the God of my salvation."*

No matter how bleak things may look, still rejoice anyway. Abram understood that despite his famine, God was still in control, and that he always takes care of his own. Verse 19 goes on to say, *"The Lord God is my strength, and he will make my feet like hind's feet, and he will make me to walk upon mine high places. To the chief singer on my stringed instruments."*

Remind you of the song by Mary McKee, and The Genesis, by any chance?

'Praise the Lord, hallelujah. I don't care what the devil's gonna do… '

One Peter 1:6, 7 says, *"Wherein you greatly rejoice, though now for a season, if need be, ye are in heaviness through manifold temptations: That the trial of your faith, being much more precious than of gold that perisheth, though it be tried with fire, might be found unto praise and honour and glory at the appearing of Jesus Christ."* God promises that whenever you pass through temptations, they won't last forever. There'll be glory at the end, as you'll certainly come out of them in the name of Jesus.

Trials and temptations are the bedrocks for building strong faith. Great adversity produced strong faith in Jacob. He experienced famine back in Canaan, but God had already gone ahead of Israel, and prepared a way through Joseph who was already in Egypt, the land of plenty.

Insurance policies and pension funds are failing today, but Abram had invested in an unfailing covenant (Genesis, 12:10). Your covenant with God will determine your lot, not the facts around you. But if that covenant isn't in place, your destiny isn't guaranteed.

So, as a result of the famine, Abram went DOWN to Egypt to settle. Egypt was the last place that should've been on his mind. Spiritually speaking, it's a place representing destruction and idolatry. Whatever situations flare up, you should never go down but up. When God sent Jonah to preach in Nineveh he rebelled and went downhill fast. Don't go down but rise up in the name of Jesus. At times, Christians need to pull each other up. So, if you go down, I pray that someone will be there to pull you up in Jesus' name.

So when the unexpected knocks on your door, don't run away. Don't draw back. Hebrews 10:39 says, *"But we are not of them who draw back unto perdition; but of them that believe unto the saving of the soul."*

Never look back. Jesus did not give in to Satan in the wilderness, and consequently we have life today. Abram went down to Egypt against God's perfect will. Thank God he never went back to Ur of Chaldees, where he came from originally. By going down to Egypt, Abram defeated himself, and achieved nothing but a lot of time wasting.

Many people delay their destinies as a result of leaving the place of their assignments. If pressure, tension and discipline don't train you—you'll never become the person God destined you to be. Discipline is what keeps you in the place of assignment. Opportunities to pack up and resign will inevitably come, but pressure should not come between you and God but should press you closer to his heart.

God doesn't want perfect people. He looks for that weak person to carry out his purposes. Matthew 7:13 says, *"Enter through the narrow gate because the gate and road that leads to destruction are wide. Many enter through the wide gate."*

If you want distress look within: if you want to be defeated look back; if you want to be distracted look around you. Preoccupation with what X or Y is doing causes distraction. But if you want to be delivered, look up to Christ.

Unfortunately, the moment pressure rises on some people, they stop coming to church, stop praying and begin to look for natural rather than spiritual solutions. The devil will scheme to make sure these solutions are temporary, with the result that you come back to church, and then three months later when another challenge arises, you start wondering is it because you came to the wrong place? Hello? Stick with God. Stick with your church.

It doesn't matter how unpleasant the new place seems to be, never go back to the place you left. Just don't do it. Don't even take advice from people that aren't godly, or who don't know the Lord Jesus Christ. Isaiah 13:1-3 says, *"Woe to the rebellious children, saith the Lord, that take counsel, but not of me; and that cover with a covering, but not of my spirit, that they may add sin to sin: They walk to go down into Egypt, and have not asked at my mouth; to strengthen themselves in the strength of Pharaoh, and to trust in the shadow of Egypt! Therefore shall the strength of Pharaoh be your shame, and the trust in the shadow of the Egypt your confusion."*

Going to the wrong place means that you will inevitably end up repeatedly doing the wrong thing. Abram, this patriarch, started lying as soon as he set foot in Egypt, the place of spiritual bondage. A lie is a lie. They don't have shades. Abraham Lincoln said that if you are going to be a liar, you must have a very good memory; otherwise you're likely to be caught out soon. One lie always leads to another.

Revelations 21:8 says that liars won't inherit the kingdom of God. Hebrews 4:13 says, *"Neither is there any creature that is not manifest in his sight: but all things are naked and opened unto the eyes of him with whom we have to do."* We serve a God of knowledge and judgement by whom all our actions are weighed.

1 Thessalonians 5:22 warns us to abstain from every appearance of evil. After Abram's compromise it wasn't long before he started to self-destruct. In Genesis 12:11, 12, he shows his willingness to give up his wife to save his own life. Worried that the Egyptians might kill him for his beautiful wife, he tells her to pretend that she is his sister, so that at the very least, his life will be preserved. He was ready to let his wife go. How selfish is that? May the Lord help us all in Jesus' name.

Just for a fleeting moment Abram forgot he was a covenant

man, and that the blessings of a whole new race was tied to his loins. Forgot that he could lose the wife that would bear the promised child. When you begin to compromise, you start behaving foolishly, including going to the wrong places, like Samson. Judges 16 records that Samson went to Gaza, where he got involved with a harlot. But then he later married Delilah, who led him to destruction not to destiny.

I'm talking to men now. Too many destinies are tied to yours for you to return to your old ways. You can't afford to misbehave again if the people looking up to you miss heaven because of your behaviour.

We go places thinking that nobody sees us, but God sees us. Proverbs 13:22 says that a good man leaves an inheritance for his children's children. That means children will reap every bad seed one sows. Do you know that you have up to three or four generations within your loins? So every time you misbehave, you are cursing unborn generations. If you understood this you'd live more responsibly, and stop committing sins, which just curses the generation after you.

Women, don't imitate Delilah's behaviour. Her constant nagging wearied Samson. What you do today will ultimately curse or bless tomorrow's generation. Ezekiel 18:2 says, *"…The fathers have eaten sour grapes, and the children's teeth are set on edge."* Parents need to understand that our children are blessed as long as we know and obey the Lord. The way that we conduct ourselves now will secure a better tomorrow for our children. They don't need to fight the battles some of us fought. We need to be prayful so that our children don't pass through what we did.

Abram's disobedience affected his whole lineage as his son, Isaac, also suffered famine (Genesis 26:1, 2). Only because of one man were the children of Israel also similarly cursed. They even kept returning to Egypt. May the Lord deliver us in Jesus' name.

His genes told him to go down to Egypt, but Isaac did the right thing after God warned him, and stayed put. Now verse 12 says, *"Then Isaac sowed in that land, and received in the same year an hundredfold: And the Lord blessed him."* So there is a way out for you when your famine comes.

Your breakthrough can never be affected by the economic situation of your country. Your breakthrough is not a function of the land, but of the open heaven upon your life, and destiny. So when you have an open heaven, you can be in the midst of famine but your needs will still be met. Isaac had an open heaven in the land of famine, and reaped a hundredfold. May that be your testimony in Jesus' name.

Nothing should drive a child of God to go back to beg from the world they left behind. If God doesn't give it then let no man give it to you, otherwise when you disobey God's will, you will end up eating sour grapes.

Why was Abram afraid to introduce Sarai as his wife in Egypt when he hadn't felt the pressure to do so in Canaan? No one had made a move on his wife there. Nor were the giants any less intimidating down in Egypt.

After they took his wife, while pretending all was well, Abram must've been sorrowful. In Genesis 12:17, divine intervention came when the Lord plagued the Egyptians so that they not only let Sarai go back to her husband, but also materially blessed them.

Despite Abram's mistake, Genesis 12:16, tells us that he got well treated. Perhaps you're living in sin? If so, just repent and turn to Jesus for help. Psalm 145:9 says that *"the Lord is good to all: and his tender mercies are over all his works"*.

God gives us richly all things to enjoy (one Timothy 6:17).

Chapter 8

ME, MYSELF AND DESTINY

At times in your life you may have asked: Why am I here? A jokey response from others may be: only God knows. But your life's no joke. God is truth: *"Who will have all men to be saved, and to come unto the knowledge of the truth"* (1 Timothy 2:4). One Corinthians 1:9 says, *"God is faithful, by whom you were called into the fellowship of his son Jesus Christ our Lord."*

Jesus Christ is not only the Truth. John 12:46 says, *"I am come a light into the world, that whosoever believeth on me should not abide in darkness".* God doesn't want us to be in the dark, but to realize there's something more to life than what our natural eyes see. In Matthew 19:16, 17, Jesus met a young, rich man, *"And, behold, one came and said unto him, Good Master, what good thing shall I do, that I may have eternal life? And he said to him, Why callest thou me good? there is none good, but one, that is, God: but if thou wilt enter into life, keep the commandments."* The commandments include seeking God's will for our lives.

God wants you and I to know his perfect will. *"And be not conformed to this world: but be ye transformed by the renewing of your mind, that you may prove what is that good, and acceptable, and perfect, will of God"* (Romans 12:2).

We have been called to destinies that may ultimately lead us to heavenly homes (see John 14:2). Destiny is divine purpose. But until you understand and also appreciate your purpose on Earth, your life will lack total joy and fulfilment. You might earn one million pounds a year, but it'll mean nothing if you don't understand your purpose here on earth.

When you know your divine purpose you'll be led to the place of your calling, which is why the devil fights tooth and nail to stop you becoming spiritually liberated from your sinful nature. He wants to keep you in bondage, emotionally, physically and materially.

But God wants to do awesome things through you; things you're totally undeserving of. That's why you've been called into his marvellous kingdom. None of us qualify for salvation, but John 3:16 tells us what we mean to him.

Abram meant a lot to God, so much that in Genesis, 15:1, 5, he said: *"Fear not, Abram: I am thy shield, and thy exceeding great reward... And he brought him forth abroad, and said, Look now toward heaven, and tell the stars, if thou be able to number them: and he said unto him, So shall thy seed be."* How humbling is that? In previous chapters we followed Abram's steps from his small beginnings, but in this chapter we'll see how he finally enters his God-ordained destiny.

Even before you were born you were ordained to walk in a divine purpose. So do you know what your destiny is? If not, you can still discover it. God is waiting for you to seek his face so he can reveal the plans and purposes he has in store for you. Jeremiah 29:11 says, *"For I know the thoughts that I think towards you, saith the Lord, thoughts of peace, and not of evil, to give you an expected end."*

So are you ready to walk into your destiny?

Genesis 3:1-4 says, *"And Abram went up out of Egypt, he, and his wife, and all that he had, and Lot with him, into the south. And Abram was very rich in cattle, in silver, and in gold. And he went on his journeys from the south, even to Bethel, unto the place where his tent had been at the beginning, between Bethel and Hai; Unto the place of the altar, which he had made there at the first: and there Abram called on the name of the Lord."*

If God tells you to stay in a place, don't budge, because you could lose more than you bargained for, as we know Abram almost lost his wife. He'd been very prosperous, yet surprisingly in Egypt, he added no profit to his wealth or health. He couldn't even say a prayer, but all that changed after he went back to where God originally wanted him.

At the end of the day, Abram's problem wasn't Canaan. It wasn't even Lot. It wasn't famine. It wasn't the devil, unbelievably. His biggest problem was himself.

Do you know that we can be our worst enemy, sometimes? Abram was already blessed but still he felt he needed to go and sojourn in Egypt. Perhaps he thought he knew better than God. That would explain why he ran ahead of God, and joined his wife's scheme to come up with a baby without

God's help. The result was Ishmael (Genesis 16), but not for very long (read Genesis 21).

You may think that you're helping God but whatever you get that's outside of God's revealed will, you'll never be able to keep. So what was Abram thinking?

If only he knew what God was thinking. *"For as the heavens are higher than the earth, so are my ways higher than your ways, and my thoughts than your thoughts."* He soon found out that God's plans for him hadn't changed after he appealed. "And Abram said unto God, O that Ishmael might live before thee!

And God said, Sarah thy wife shall bear thee a son, indeed; and thou shalt call his name Isaac: and I will establish my covenant with him for an everlasting covenant, and with his seed after him.

And as for Ishmael, I have heard thee: Behold, I have blessed him, and will make him fruitful, and will multiply him exceedingly; 12 princes shall he beget, and I will make him a great nation.

But my covenant will I establish with Isaac, which Sarah shall bear unto thee at this set time in the next year.

And he left off talking with him, and God went up from Abram" (Genesis 17:18-22).

Isn't God just too good? Even if we go off track, he stays on track. No wonder James 1:17 says, "Every good gift and every perfect gift is from above, and cometh down from the Father of lights, with whom there is no variableness, neither shadow of turning." Though Abram coming to his senses and deciding to go back helped, God would've still carried out his purposes anyway.

How many of us are prepared to humble ourselves and do similar U turns for all the wrong decisions we've made? Wouldn't we rather ignore our consciences and stay in the apparent comfort zone of Egypt, much like Lot choosing to stay in Sodom and Gomorrah (Genesis 13), but not for very long (see Genesis 14).

We can often choose between God's perfect or permissible will, but I know which one I'd want, if it meant receiving God's best and not settling for second best (see Matthew 19:3-8, for example). Once you overcome your own will, nothing can stop your destiny.

Romans 8:28, 30 says, *"And we know that all things work together for good to them that love God, to them who are called according to his purpose. For whom he did foreknow, he also did predestinate to be conformed to the image of his Son, that he might be the firstborn among many brethren. Moreover whom he did predestinate, them he also called, and whom he called, them he also justified; and whom he justified, them he also glorified."*

All the things that work together relates to the good, the bad, and the ugly in our lives. So that includes losing your job, your car breaking down or someone injuring you by mistake or intentionally. Even after you've gone for that second job interview, only to receive 'It is with regret' - all things work together. Choose to live by these foundations, and all will be well.

All things work together for my good was what Joseph told himself when he was wrongly imprisoned. But what if you're arrested for wrongdoings? As long as you repent and undergo God's corrections during your incarceration, all things still work together for your good if you continue to love God.

Knowledge is power, and ignorance is loss, not bliss. Proverbs 29:18 says, *"Where there is no vision: the people perish: but he that keepeth the law, happy is he."* So where there's no revelation, people die. Where there's no understanding, people perish. Some of us were meant to be going to Birmingham and found ourselves in Bedford, because Birmingham didn't seem to have prospects.

Spiritual foresight enables you to see potential in anything, but some of us fail to see potential in the things God does. Regardless of your mistakes, God still chooses to see potential in you even after people have written you off.

God wants you to become a star in his kingdom. His vision for Abram meant taking him spiritually to another country. It's important to understand that for your vision to manifest you have to be in the right place at the right time. You weren't designed for helter-skelter living. Your life should have direction and purpose.

You will languish when you lack insight of God's will for your life. But all things are possible to visionaries (see Matthew 19:26, Mark 9:23). A vision of destiny motivates you to accomplish a better future. But where there's no revelation of a better tomorrow, people perish. Where there is no revelation of tomorrow being better than your present, you will live hopelessly.

Perish also means nakedness. Thus, a lack of vision or destination exposes you, but nobody will know your nakedness in Jesus' name. Another meaning is to uncover. May your secret not be uncovered in Jesus' name. It also refers to casting off restraints. Today, the lack of restraint in society, has led to soaring crime, sexual immorality and resultant diseases.

John 13:31 says, *"...Jesus said, Now is the Son of man glorified, and God is glorified in him."* Christianity involves our going from one level of glory to another. It has nothing to do with 'Abracadabra'. You can't wave a magic wand and get instantaneous success. Rather, you have to start from somewhere. You don't begin to give today and expect to get back a multiple harvest, tomorrow.

Matthew 6:33 says, *"But seek ye first the kingdom of God, and his righteousness; and all these things shall be added unto you."* Things mean additional extras. So when God can trust you with £10, he'll give you £20. When you can be trusted with £50, he'll give you £100. But when you've failed to manage £10, don't expect God to bless you with £1 million.

You must pass through addition before you can receive multiplication. God takes us through a process, so that when we have £1 million, we can appreciate the person who only has £10. Make up your mind to increase your giving even if it's just by a penny. Say, this month I'll give one pound, next month, £1.20 or as the Lord leads. Now when you do that, you're adding gradually, and God will begin to multiply back to you whatever you give. That's why I often tell people that if they don't learn to increase their offerings, they could be delaying more blessings.

Are you delaying destiny?

You've got to understand that the devil will try to hijack your spiritual progress like he tried to with Moses. He tempted Pharaoh to kill every male child born under a certain age, but thank God, Moses survived to live out his great purpose in life. If you've survived problems until now, it's because of God's purpose for your life. If it hadn't been for his purpose, you might not even be living now.

I remember being involved in a car accident in my childhood. A car drove over my legs yet I was unharmed, thank God. But if my legs had been broken, I wouldn't be walking today. There is a future for you and me, in the name of Jesus. Revelations 4:11 tells us that we were created for his pleasure.

Joshua fulfilled his remarkable destiny but he could have died along with the rest of the children of Israel in the wilderness. You too will fulfil your own in Jesus' name. Herod killed countless babies, in his attempt to kill the vision of a Saviour King. The boy Jesus became an Egyptian fugitive. He had to run. Sometimes when led by God it's Ok to run from dangerous situations. Two Timothy 2:22 says, *"Flee also youthful lusts: but follow righteousness faith, charity, peace, with them that call on the Lord out of a right heart."* One Corinthians 6:18 also says, "Flee fornication…"

You have been given spiritual goals that must be achieved during your lifetime. That's what predestination is. The common purpose of born again Christians is to glorify God, so you must always conduct your life to that purpose.

After you realize that it's no longer about me, myself, and I - the evil trinity of self (2 Timothy 3:1, 2), but me: myself, and destiny - you will walk into your destiny.

Chapter 9

IS YOUR OPPORTUNITY
KNOCKING?

Somebody once said that opportunity comes but fleetingly. So rare is it that many of us often miss it when it comes. But isn't it reassuring to know that we serve a God of second chances? Nevertheless, if we aren't looking for opportunities we can miss them. If that were not the case, then many of us wouldn't have recourse to think about what-might-have-been, or, the if-onlys...

Many blind people are visionaries. They wrote some of the great hymns we sing in church today. But what could be worse than blindness is to have sight but lack vision. To have sight, but lack vision is the worst thing that could happen to human beings. Abram had Ishmael by Hagar after a momentary lapse of vision. May you not lack vision in Jesus' name.

The main point of what I'm saying here is that true visionaries seize opportunities when they come.

Will you grab your opportunity when it comes knocking?

Or will you be in the wrong place, at the wrong time?

In my early days, I was given an opportunity to serve in a church, yet had I rejected it for any reason, perhaps I wouldn't be here today, and you wouldn't be reading this book.

But guess what? I'm doing what I was created to do. This is why God made me.

This is God's purpose for my life, yet all too easily; I could have been languishing as a medical doctor, taking out my frustration on patients and colleagues. That's no life, making everybody's lives miserable because I'm in the wrong place. That's definitely not what God created you to do.

But if that's what you are like, it's not too late to walk away today. God gave Noah an opportunity to walk away when he told him to build the Ark, and he obeyed while the whole world laughed and despised him. When the flood came, he was afloat. May your vision be afloat in the name of Jesus.

As soon as you become a visionary, expect opportunities to come at the most seemingly inopportune times. Opportunity knocked for Esther. One day was all she had to make a life changing choice. While the clock ticked the lives of the Jewish nation hung in the balance.

"Then Mordecai commanded to answer Esther, Think not with

88

thyself that thou shalt escape in the king's house, more than all the Jews. For if thou altogether holdest thy peace at this time, then shall there enlargement and deliverance arise to the Jews from another place; but thou and thy father's house shall be destroyed: and who knoweth whether thou art come to the kingdom for such a time as this?" Esther 4:13, 14

Be prepared to listen to godly counsel. Esther wouldn't have done the right thing without it. Her predecessor, Queen Vashti was ousted for being proud. Learn from other people's mistakes. Habakkuk 2:4 says, *"Behold, his soul which is lifted up is not upright in him: but the just shall live by his faith."* You can't fulfil God's divine purpose with a prideful attitude. James 4:6 says, "But he giveth more grace. Wherefore he saith, God resisteth the proud, but giveth grace to the humble."

You must understand that in order to get to destiny, you'll need to come from a place of humility. You may be a regular churchgoer, but do you help out in any way or are you a time waster? If you're just wasting space, you're holding back your destiny.

There's always something to do in a church. Look out for opportunities even if there don't appear to be any. Perhaps you could join an intercessor's group, or learn to play a musical instrument. Some churches are lacking in certain instruments. Why not buy a harp or a harmonica, get some lessons, and then bless the church with your musical gift?

You'll have joy in life, and a sense of fulfilment, but you can't have that until you understand what Heaven created you to do. What Heaven created you to do will ultimately bring you to glorification.

Abram was doing well in Ur of the Chaldees, but opportunities to fulfil his destiny weren't realistic there. So God had to put him in a new place.

Where Abram was now able to fulfil his purpose on the earth. Can you guess what that was?

To start a new generation!

Genesis 21:1, 2 says, *"And the Lord visited Sarah as he had said, and the Lord did unto Sarah as he had spoken. For she conceived, and bear Abram a son in his old age, at the set time of which God had spoken to him."*

The set time is when an opportunity comes knocking that will usher you into your divine purpose. May you not miss your set time in the name of Jesus. Romans 8:18 says, *"For I reckoned that the sufferings of this present time are not worthy to be compared with the glory that shall be revealed in us. For the earnest expectation of the creature waiteth for the manifestation of the sons of God."* Your God-given vision is always bigger than you., and means that a new generation is waiting on you to fulfil destiny.

But maybe you let opportunities go because you thought you were too small?

You're not on your own. Moses thought the same thing: *"And Moses said unto God, Who am I?"* Exodus 3:11

Perhaps someone downsized your vision or opportunity?

Perhaps you've been in the wilderness for so long that you think that God has forgotten you. I want to remind you of

Ecclesiastes 3:1, *"To everything there is a season, and a time to every purpose under the Heaven."* Nothing ever happens to us by mistake. Remember, God has your lives in his hands.

It may seem that you're sowing in vain, but don't despair, Psalm 30:5 says, *"Weeping may endure for a night, but joy cometh in the morning."* Psalms 126:6 also says, *"He that goeth forth and weepeth, bearing precious seed, shall doubtless come again with rejoicing, bringing his sheaves with him."* Precious seeds apply to weeping, and sheaves means laughter.

Job said that all the days of my appointed time would I wait, till my change comes. He knew that a change was inevitable. Job 14:7 says, *"For there is hope of a tree, if it be cut down, that it will sprout again, and that the tender branch thereof will not cease."*

So your change is inevitable.

An opportunity is surely coming your way.

So rejoice with others when they seize their opportunity of a lifetime, because others will rejoice with you when your time comes. No wonder Romans 12:15 says, we should rejoice with those that rejoice, and weep with those that weep.

After you've passed through, your change will come in Jesus' name. It may not look like it today. But your change is imminent. Be patient and wait, as James 5:7 says, *"Be patient therefore, brethren, unto the coming of the Lord. Behold, the husbandman waiteth for the precious fruit of the earth and hath long patience for it, until he receive the early and latter rain."* God is never late.

I hear an opportunity knocking for someone. May it be for you in Jesus' name.

Chapter 10

YOUR SPIRITUAL CHECKLIST

You'll need to follow in Abram's steps if you're going to secure your destiny, (just don't go down to Egypt!). That means you'll need to:

1.   Be born again. Get into a relationship with Jesus (John 1:12, 3:16, 15:16).

2. · Consistently obey God's instructions and commandments (Isaiah 1:19, Job 36:11-12).

3.   Don't compromise ever. Never compromise the standards that God has set you as a child of God. (Ephesians 4:1, Luke 9:62)

4.   Always firstly call upon the Lord, for divine intervention on your behalf (Jeremiah 33:3, Luke 18:1, James 5:12-16, Psalm 62:1, 2).

What to do when the unexpected happens?

1.   Never lose sight of God (Hebrews 12:2).

2.   Learn to rejoice! (Hebrews 3:17-19, Habakkuk 3:17-19).

3.   Stay in your place of calling (Ecclesiastes 10:4).

4.   Refuse to be swayed by the facts around you (2 Corinthians 4:18).

5.   Be continually thankful (one Thessalonians 5:17, 18).

6.   Meditate on the Word (Joshua 1:8). Expect solutions to come your way!

7.   Wait like David who never moved until he heard from God. (Psalms 123: 2, Isaiah 40:31)

8.   Know your seasons (Ecclesiastes 3:1-12, Psalm 30:5). Your victory is around the corner.

9.   Realise that every temptation is meant for you to enjoy supernatural provision (Philippians 1:12).

ABOUT SHINING LIGHT GROUP

The Shining Light Group was born out of desire and call of God to impact knowledge to mankind through biblical and life teaching experiences.

We take our inspiration from Proverbs 4: 18, which says, "But the path of the just is as a shining light, that shineth more and more unto the perfect day.

We are committed not only to helping people identify their God given gift and potentials, but also guided by a policy to follow through to ensure individual vision are realised.

The SLG is a ministry with purposeful mission. Our audience cuts across denominations, religion and philosophical barrier. We are everything to all people.

Our tools for reaching out includes newsletters, motivational and personal development books, and publication, audio and video materials.

Shining Light Group
Connection Point
1-9 Sewell Street, Plaistow London
E13 8AT
Tel: 020 8552 8822 Fax: 020 852 8823
Email: info@shininglightgroup.com

www.shininglightgroup.com

NOTES

NOTES

NOTES

NOTES

NOTES